I0618677

Into

Into

Poetry by
Christopher Sweeney/Robert Snyderman/Lonely Christopher

Seven CirclePress

Into by Christopher Sweeney/Robert Snyderman/Lonely Christopher
2010 Seven CirclePress 1st Edition

This work is licensed under the Creative Commons Attribution-
Noncommercial 3.0 United States License. To view a copy of this
license, visit http://creativecommons.org/licenses/by-nc/3.0/us/ or send
a letter to Creative Commons, 171 Second Street, Suite 300, San
Francisco, California, 94105, USA.

You are free to reuse/redistribute the works herein under the terms of
the above mentioned license.
In case of reuse/redistribution please attribute to:
*Into by Christopher Sweeney/Robert Snyderman/Lonely Christopher
2010 Seven CirclePress 1st Edition.*
Failure to make proper acknowledgements will result in loss of re-
use/redistribution rights and may lead to legal action.
For further permissions including but not limited to commercial use
please contact the publisher (who in turn will contact the authors) at:
editor-in-chief@sevencirclepress.com.

Published by Seven CirclePress: A Homegrown Literary Venue
Help Support Grass-Roots Literature Visit: www.sevencirclepress.com

ISBN 13: 978-0-615-35054-7

Contents

Introduction

Into brings together three young poets who, at first glance, have nothing to do with one another. They belong to no common school or movement; they share no political program or artistic sensibility; they frequently cannot even agree on the purpose and meaning of their craft. It would be vain to look for ties of borrowing or influence between them. Where one embraces formalism and abstraction, another clings to materiality. Where one stands apart from tradition, another takes refuge in it. Where one places his own subjectivity at the center of his work, another elides himself entirely.

And yet this collection was not assembled by chance. The poets represented here—Christopher Sweeney, Robert Snyderman, and Lonely Christopher—have maintained, for all the differences in their thinking, a deep and long-lasting creative collaboration. Together they have created and sustained settings in which poetry and other arts could be presented, discussed, and experienced. For years, they hosted a biweekly salon at their Brooklyn apartment, providing dozens of emerging writers and poets with a platform and an audience for their work; more recently, they have been among the founders of a press which aims, through its journal Correspondence as well as other publications, to serve the same end in a durable medium. Their efforts are animated by an imperative sense of the need to preserve and cultivate the openness of poetry to the irruption of new voices and projects. It is in this spirit that this book is offered.

Christopher Sweeney, whose poem "Face" opens this volume, has been preoccupied for a long time with the question of the possibilities of poetry. In his early work, he often placed the emphasis on the problem's political valences: the poet appeared inevitably as a combatant, the bearer of resistance to the monolith of state power and corporatized culture. Gradually, this messianic impulse has given way to a nuanced understanding of the interpenetration of poetry and philosophy. Sweeney is especially influenced by Martin Heidegger, who envisions the poet as occupying a privileged position of access to unchanging and ineffable Being. Yet this position is not taken for granted in Sweeney's work. Rather, the poet's role in the world—and its potentially liberating or mystical implications—

is always treated as a problem, one which can be approached most closely by and within the medium itself. His poems are accordingly not about his own clarity of insight and profundity of vision; they deal instead with hesitation, confusion, and obscurity, the doors of perception never quite becoming cleansed.

To Robert Snyderman, the author of "The Mountain," belongs the credit for conceiving and assembling this book. Snyderman is perpetually peripatetic; over the past couple of years, he has crisscrossed both Canada and the United States. This accounts, perhaps, for the frenetic quality of the verse, the persistent feeling of being woken up in the middle of the night. But the poem's spare and unyielding structure is also the outcome of a complex creative trajectory. At the beginning of his practice as a poet, Snyderman made the nature of spoken and written expression one of his central themes; the reconciliation of the interiority and exteriority of subjective experience through expression seemed to him effectively impossible. Eventually, his work in theater and playwriting helped him develop a performative, storytelling style, in which the poet's voice could become completely transformed by his subject—and with that development came a growing interest in the chasm that separates performance from communication. The result of the latter was a series of major poems brought together under the title Cloth, constituting, in effect, a simultaneous performance of poetry and of poetry's impossibility. "The Mountain" continues this development, for, as he has always defined it, "The Mountain is what does not write." More than any other one of his poems, this one is a set of jottings, of increasingly sparse field notes in a journey that leads away from writing.

Lonely Christopher's poems "The House of There Is" and "The Great Bird Will Take the Universe" complete the volume. Christopher—unlike Sweeney and Snyderman—has always treated the gap between text and reality as a subject for irony rather than despair. His earliest compositions relied on a playful authorial dissociation from the subject matter, experimenting freely with rhetorical and narrative postures of various kinds. Soon he began to think more seriously about exploiting the resources of this gap. Discarding the question of reality completely, Christopher produced texts in which writing was reduced to a pile of basic components—decontextualized words, sounds, and letters. Most recently, he has centered his creative process on techniques of détournement and reappropriation, which serve to undermine literature's aura of authenticity and dethrone the author himself. ("The House of There Is" is composed, through selective cropping, from Jonathan Edwards's sermon "Sinners in the Hands of an Angry God"; "The Great Bird Will Take the Universe," from Freud's essay on Leonardo da Vinci's homosexuality.)

Questions of identity are also central to Christopher's work. As an emerging queer writer and playwright, he has been searching for ways to deploy his stylistics in the service of his sexuality, without, however, renouncing his stance on the nature of texts or becoming part of the mainstream of gay literature. The ambiguities inherent in such a project are suggested even by his poems in this book. If the death of the subject is a constant refrain in "The House of There Is," it is because both the explicit message and the ironic distancing effect of the plagiarism technique conspire with one another and agree. In "The Great Bird Will Take the Universe," the poem and the technique are at odds: the one is a painful and disillusioned narrative of queer identity, while the other implicitly denies that any such sincerity can be possible.

All three of our poets, in a sense, have independently of one another arrived at a similar impasse. Sweeney is unable to bridge the gap between the supposed clairvoyant insight of the poet and the obscured terrain of everyday reality; Snyderman, that between poetry and the inadequacy of the word; Christopher, that between the imperative of identity and the emptiness at the heart of the text. But, just as we can sense slippery intimations of the problem in each poem ("losing, but what; what?" asks "Face"), so we can see, sketched out on the sand, something almost like a solution. The last section of "Face," after the mournful penultimate one, is a breath of fresh air: "if the ocean/would come with you, /scuttling/awake again/like an old dog,/some insistent azure/weighting/on the otherwise/free arms,//we are home again."

In "Great Bird," too, something of a resolution is afoot. The problem of the detachment (the revelation of the emptiness) brought about by plagiarism is relevant for us only if we think of the poem as an act of defiance, a queer narrative wrought out of a homophobic text. On one level, of course, it is that. But on another, both the poem and its foil the original are in fact rendered powerless by the vulture—the "great bird," which stands in for the origin of sexuality in human experience. "The moment of being/

experienced and afterward repeated is already past/in the process of writing history." Neither text can recover this moment, which, as the title suggests, will take the universe. It stands at the empty center, inaccessible by language, as the poet's strange queer secret.

For Snyderman, the way in is also the way out. The long creative arc that is completed, in a sense, by "The Mountain" is one in which the overriding concern is the problem of not-writing. "The Mountain" offers a surprisingly blunt riposte: "Time writes." The sense of materiality, movement, and place that has always animated Snyderman's poetry becomes incarnate in the literary form of a voyage. The writing itself is thus not the conscious act of a deliberately poetizing subject but the record, inscribed by some other hand, of a series of movements across the mountain's surface. While the poet traverses, ascends, and descends, the rocky periphery of not-writing, time writes "The Mountain" itself. "Who constantly departs from the Mountain/is who I found alive"—that is, it seems, Snyderman himself.

-Greg Afinogenov

Face

by Christopher Sweeney

I

Except that one
seizes you to slough
off the rain; accept
that you are not
there. Into doorcrack
elevate tower; syllable to
syllable entranched
sluice to circumfluence;
that the real rain glut
the channel, made
a symbol of it.

Defend the sentence;
hold it back.
Against nothing becomes
likewise, whereto,
wherefore? Take it
in place; ventriloquate,
make it say something.
The details forgotten
create. That we had
to do something, we
took it in place.
Since there would be
an idol, sought one
with stature, meeting
you where the earth
isn't earnest or kind.

Hammered on
scornfully—
black, like the
wheel's black,
decay splayed
in the shadows' breaks—
breaking
that absolved form.

Concrete, stone rubble,
rut; you led,
the car fleeing
over
imperiled oak
arms;

the ash on machine parts
and chaff;
weave of trees
with giant iron
legs, decayed
like a mangled cloth.

And the car skidded wide
into the mudruts,
the almost bare
stanchion stood;
had juniper covered the cold
sweating slab; invariably
who left, they were
who left; would not
that the lights
turn in, and
the stare.

When
couldn't have lifelessly
like now,

where it is brighter in the not knowing,

trace the time to a midpoint
and say of breakage,
there—

with
the blurring of the blue-white dress
and the blond torrent of the dying grass,

I was stopped,

thoughtlessly,

A shallow of bread,
breath
cold straying
the car window

and coming up,
under the framing
ghostly oaks,
something
almost holy:
light breaking
onto the road
the road
breaking
to ocean.

Yard,
roaming
of the almost trains,
horn. Then metal

out of the dust
breach—
your call
cawing over the trestle.

Tepid stagger
maintained
at the internecine,
stoplessly
drawing
away;

And you were who
attended
my other windows, once

once,

Oncoming diamonds
of light
like procession
of the haloed faces
blooming.
Everything was very wide
and then the light became
depeopled.

Crack into the
cold hole—
if it were raging—
but still small;
little voice,
we'll go home
again; accept
that you are not there.

Cowling
into the wetshed
from
the what coming.

Our piteous
possession,
our last

hold;

II

With follow me,
to be with me
here, name
the uncovered
waste of
this place
with a meal

if calcined
are these stuffy
containers, as
to tarry a little.

Who would believe it
being here, to
rasp in a muttering
consort, heaving
speech in air—

Companile
pealed from her crowds
to dawn to who
would greet the
ganglia of a spent
day, such her
interjection through
the lawns; builds
that is stone,
pebble slag, and—
matrix that downs
the eyes; follow me,
shines, that forms
crammed column.

From the rain-tower,
unto two clumsy jaws,
we were weaned,
needfully gnashing—

two, likely lying
in the letter's
aliment—we were
slowly hollowed
of our raining parliament;
hastening to harvest
the same nourishing word—

cottage waits
somewhat loyally
in the permanent
future; way ranges
savagely
for those, despite all,
trying to write
here.

You wept to the
bleach wet;
waking in no home
arch-longing to the third,
even ultimate
tomorrow.

There, unhoping
if briefly,
back to the sheets wet
and the feet sobbing,
halting
through the paint hall
defiant
into time,
looming.

Soft covetous hands,
fury, that the place
is the wrong place
as the product
of time. No
bower, but a mutilate
plain, a fire broken alley
and what if fate
had fated us the wrong
thing: whatever
was engaged that night
in the tremulous rain
was hope, hope
in the right way.

Soft covetous hands,
fury: fleck of
beauty, an
impossible way,
and the place,
which is the wrong place,
perpetuates pain; but
like a tree ascending
and over extending
you were and would
rather be: pile

of groaning embers,
limbs ripping
in a scream,
would rather be stamped out

or felled and withering heap,
than traveling all night,
as it would otherwise be.

Place perpetuates pain
and confine impotent, broods;
where running
was iterate forth,
nothing came of it.

As you were and
would rather be;
there was nothing better to offer.

Corroborate one lodestar
into its untenable place:
sitting cross-legged
in a smoky container,
where the flooding
world wouldn't believe
us.

To sit with you there,
as if that would be;
you would serve the
burnt entrails of an
old potato as if you
were someone. And what
if you let a line foment
around its beginnings, as
if the union of breakfasts
would finally point
somewhere? As if you
could just have it. Afford
a year mellifluous passage;
to work was two hours,

while you slept, trembling.

Who
attested, most of all,
so powerfully—
who led
sleeplessly
out
from the tower
with rain:

place constricts
obliquely;—

testament
into the numberless
now, tunnel.

III

No charm to disenchant,
nor airy reflection
on pond water;

sour limbs
raffled together
in this place,

secretive, visible
arms
harbor
the little flesh;
simple, a silvery

breath
silicifies,
which must,
or two bark
drift,
numb and drift.

Sew into my
hands

to make it all
more tangible;

into the skin
if it remains,
and only thus.

Slink into the
sidewalk furrows—
you were
trembling fists—
some saline
that would drain
away you,
begging for
both's sake—I
also—

Hammering
into a too-dark
future
with the word
salvage;
hoisting and
plying
from the
as-dark past;
as if
we could turn
around,
sideways,
and slip
into the
different
glittering current.

Door creaking
clove quietly shuttered.
From my sheet's opening:
shuddering under
your cigarette smoke,
entered: everyone slept;
undressed
because no one
was listening.
Down the paint hall,
the wet sock
traces of rain,

and since space
is in time
being hunted away—
under the smoke,
unsuspected,
shuddering, twine,

stray-playing
out from the blankets—.

Only in secret:
prefer waking.

And whatever you have,
hold; and if that
is two pain knots,
barricade—that
feet quicken to mire
into mossy circuits,
that the rain appointed
only that muddy
bower—do not abandon
that belief, simply
because it wasn't|
true; and if you, again,
would gather words
together, onto the
three uncrumbling
blocks, let that
sentence be as
little honest as the
month of May—not
that we were then
reposed, by what
affords no guerdon
but that a little
buckling transverse would
narrate together
the gravel; let there
be a story with you up
to the gate;

valley and fable
arraigned—

keeper, deceive.

Womb, untimelessly;
twine
buckled in the before snow.
I think the voices
of friends
were calling.

Warm. We were very quiet.

The ashes:
I had been there—
scarefully; and
you,
you—light
down the fire open
alley,
feet wet,
it had been
your hall,
your bedroom;
you
brazenly—the swampy
bedroom;

there is nothing
left,
vague breasts.
Behind the
sink,
you left
that
in the old kitchen.

We went—
brittle
as time's run,
cracking over the stony surface:
meaningless wields on—

to the fire
which was very meek;
water sputtered off
cliff's end.

Cowered—the hearth
was trying to invite.
Our hands trembled
as guests.
From the other way
voices came, reflected
the light. Wine was,
and someone was brave
like a laugh.
Because there is rain,
time ends; and because
we had no hollow—

footsteps through trees' alley,
a few leaves—
there was no sky.
Wet,
stumbling underbrush,
it came
that the one before me

wasn't
more than darkness—.

Foot path dispersed,
and when there is only sound;

Light was coming;
alone, three last miles
over open ground.

Because the river was, the bridge—
then,
light was; it was

something thinkable.

There was the one who once babbled,
—long, down, at the end of the hall—
resolved into a cleft in shapes;

first: learning to use words
by the rusted machinery, or still—

first, your word was,
that: where the rain was,

under
what pretended to be time's tower.

Water: autumn-cold,
so in
to the warm dark
where babble would,
but not then, then
blankets were,

and word's weak, coming.

Light, we went where the light was;
rain again and very far. Road,
stone-rubble, rut.

What was a gate?
Stanchion, lattice—said,
this, further—
no; would I have known

that, almost, as how the river swallows
it would—no, not this
gate, there was none—
go to word's end,
further.

Those terrible braids of steel,
there, where dwindled
to the last two halos of light.

A first death might be very brief,
months, barely. Somehow,
there was always rain but—.

Middle: bleach tears;
and then in the numerous warm dark
right before time didn't fizzle
when there had been snow,
mythless, would persist,
in the array of bottles as the walls spoke
until,
very dim, the room denuded,
sat, we two—

in, through the narrow of the tunnel of night,
gate? what gate?
Each far, further; but then over the iron,
beyond the almost train,
cleaving at cliff's lip—engrafted.

Because the river was, the bridge
then,
light was; it was

something thinkable.

Recoiled, the cracking
seam of the jaw,
no thought—sudden,
two revolutions
and the floor;
fled,
down
the narrowing
concave—
if home soons,
if the blanket warm
would; perhaps time,
water? Because sense
which sudden spites
broke straight,
because
straight burdened
into heap,
learning to use words,
the world gets the better of you:

flight's end meant ceramic scree:
scrap blanket book;
losing, but what;
what? leaving.
Shattered the night shaft
yet into darker pieces;
wake, if beyond a form of waking,
wake.

Concave went the curve of your saying
under words'
winnower
until there were three,

and babble—if times,
standing,

what,
what was my name?
Under the three's dark rill of babble—
if times, standing—.

Recoiled down hall's end,
dissolved beyond shapes.

IV

If from a tracery
of shale and foam,
bellowing, with brine and breeze,
you traversed the shoals,
and if the ocean
would come with you,
scuttling
awake again
like an old dog,
some insistent azure
weighting
on the otherwise
free arms,

we are home again;
scud, wisping
to disperse
again: congreet
radiate, on.

The Mountain

by Robert Samuel Snyderman

"to sing in the wilderness toward God"
                    Allen Ginsberg, Kaddish

I tore my arms off

not to warn   but to pass.
Fire is for heat.

Yuliya and I had climbed a tree in Prospect Park in Brooklyn in
September.

I bought new clothes oh new clothes
to naked devote my earthen placement

Oppression becomes satire.

Our future is a sensitive eyelid. The first child.

                                        I wanted
  dominance.

But   to write but,   human life.
                          hole
                     half
              the mountain

with her
                          leave
the mountain tames none
    of his eyes   you

        face   limbs   beckon
                                                      all

                                            thoughts
    me the body   the
                                      not wanting to wear

                          the   the north america by hand
                                                  father leaping off
you will leave   a   white shadows
                     source
        of the   stamina   perhaps back
    in pursuit of   in
        also   fire?
    an is tamed no one   man

        summoned   self
    hands of
one summoned
                                                      until rough

an eye that is also

                                            Monotone aurora that
        to a hole in her face   Flesh is terse and will not

break but with time or extreme

viciousness that I bite my hand

and can not break its flesh or

mind drowned in fear of youth in
youth.

In my sleep why keep us?

Zeide disappeared between the eyes,

with a labyrinth.

Criminal

!   Legs crossed. Legs stuffed with bodies.

What is a first man? He did not bring clothes with him.
Enough is enough. No compass
and roads leave.

I must walk.

I see who inherited.

I see who inherited.

The magnified man does not create.

Time writes.

Your arrogance   Dehydration   Shadow

The Halfdance:

        say this
       under me:
   nomad's natural disas ter.

      I want controlled nomads to listen too.

      Spit on the mountain.
                  Storytellers.

                              Left town, I so oblivion
                              winter sweat north.
            So I began
                         hand writing this book.
            So I made my tongue.

I am an animal. I have never suffocated before.

I keep awake with opening and shutting.

        I kneeled. I crowded, crowded, born into 22 years again and
again to establish property.
To bless.
                         To
father.   This is

    the fat of silence

FEBRUARY   this is denied death.

The mountain is an annex.

I remember it.

                    Unslept
his bowels in the plum tree of a mountainous threshold

                                        eyefull,

ins ide a sound   my   has   disappeared and the hair behind

            head been chopped sculpted doused and painted on
            inside a sound, as   if   inside a vandal.

Written woman woman written.

      Ear   body,
       join me

                          traveling North

Into was to begin.

What falls follows?
The body's book.

The Mountain will or will not.
The Mountain must be confronted,

I can, I say hacked in. I say hacked into two nurtured peaks.

Two nurtured peaks   protect you. You not want more than one warning.

Storytellers.
Burners.

My absent companion

is like a tyranny of tyranny of arriving bodies.
                    In the sskull of a brain.

        springautumn   The question was born to confront
                                                    and I found it in an eye
                                                        before a tree
                                                          in a field
                                                    outside the fence
                                                      of a cemetery
                                                    in New York state
                                              with Christopher Sweeney
                                                surrounded by deer.

Drinkers of daylight.

Then root

the voice of mutant harnessed,
            the sound the wind inside his legs.

        Cold fire to speak
                        so speak   if I have not avoided weathering,
                spun pregnant   if not this   book crucified into the
doors of houses.

I will offer you myself.

I stay.

Disease, religion,
hallucination is the keeping of that you cannot carry sickness,
detachment
torn pregnant
into a deathdance.

A tongue to write with an eye to shut an eye to shut an eye to at
to at and open to tear at as if willing to enter as willing to
enter.
Willing to enter and confronted them as if willing and come upon
them and this book they carried and the eye they carried protected
them in their sleep as if willing.
You will need what they will need if not needed of them as if willing
as if needed of you.

February 14 2009
      who
      refuses to
      visit. who would not abandon. Wake my chest. Is
      where with two names, one
      names self, and does not name what does not exile,
is who does not exile. cannot.

February 15 2009
      Who constantly departs from the Mountain
is who I found alive.

I awoke descending. I awoke ascending.

The insomnia that measures judgment

it is not confusion

an eye that is also light

The House of There Is

by Lonely Christopher

In this verse is
threatened vengeance
not withstanding
understanding
under all the text

being represented
destruction
expected destruction
all that stands shall fall

the reason already
appointed time
from the words
but is not so
so there is
no defense
what is
ends

earth trembles
destroy nothing
hold it back

place is the sentence
objects of wrath
why not because
angry and quiet because

because
represents waiting
swallowed up and lost
corrupt principles are violent
break out after the manner

the troubled power
for the present
is destructive

no security
by any accident

there is danger in circumstances
experience is no evidence
there are
places so weak these places
are not seen

death has so many ways
all means are there
and so
and so

the world is universally subject
determination means
universal experience

what has done
in what is now doing
to do
matters nothing
doing
is but shadow

the part that means
was not there because
it did not matter
the subject
if it were so
came not to be

death dreams
it makes
sudden destruction
then there would be
pleasing promises
but for that death
makes no promises

all the promises
have no interest

manifest under no manner
a moment from eternal destruction
so that thus it is

this sentence suffering
done nothing
in anger any promise
would swallow up hearts
break out
there are no means

nothing preserves every moment
the arbitrary use
is nothing
only power

things as other
constitution means
these things
are nothing
no more subject

don't shine
don't yield
upon air
maintain purpose
abuse the subject
abuse the end

the present
more and more
higher and higher

time is mean
constantly increasing
wrath would

rush forth
it would

nothing is bent
nothing is promised
a promise
is drunk blood

dead
unexperienced light
has no form
nothing but this moment
swallows destruction

however gone
from being
destruction expects nothing
things are nothing
but air and
empty shadows

nothing else
nothing but
no other reason
there is no other reason

to be gone
is
the house of there is

nothing else given
against it
about it

every moment
and nothing
save nothing
is done
nothing to spare nothing

one moment

things are in such danger
wrath it is
wrath the most

the subject rages
an arbitrary fury this
is nothing less
than nothing

love is terrible
and after that
no more
will come after that
but that with fire
to render places
and the words
are terrible

what will become
shall suffer
there shall be no
way

nothing shall be
because it's so hard
now the day
will be in vain
awful words are words
in blood

impossible words
great manifestations
things cry from that
crush out blood
make it fly
hate the place
misery to that end

love is punishment
time was before
destruction is
design

infinite terribleness
is presence
one moment
against forever
a duration before

manner is what remains
representation is this
congregation that has
all but the subject
what an awful thing
what an awful congregation

time now sits quiet
time will come in
perfect despair

the house
would not
give conditions
with blood
to cause
such conditions there

nothing is done
any manner is extremely
dangerous
the present
will soon be
blindness
and hardness

angry night

and happy word
increases guilt
and never was
so great
a danger there

being
and blindness
seem bigger
now in time

the rest will be blinded
the rest
will curse the day

gone is the manner
that is there
this congregation
consumed by
the end

The Great Bird Will Take the Universe

by Lonely Christopher

I

When researches, normally
                    blacken the sublime
ascribe material for these reasons
objects that concern   everything
recognized—unpublished development in him:
        severe in the end, according to the words
        his failure art.
What prevented the cause?
Remarkable architect
unusual refinement. It is indeed quite possible
activity, security, form of research
dead bodies and human beings—flying machines.
        Distorted vestiges, experimental attempts:
his works excuses
then days would pass.
The evidence is seen to be a symptom. Technical
miscarriage
which he left unfinished,   building
contradictions. A certain everyone   at a time.
        Pleasure described this feminine
        deprive animals. Study good and
evil. Biographical hero's mental
following sentence.   Pretty writing
posthumous problems.   A struggle
artist   surprise everything sexual.
        Womb
never embraced a woman in passion—
        as a model he surrounded
        his death was named without sharing.
Existence did not extend to sexual activity.
        There is way emotional
        scientific problem
        the way writers in plastic terms.
His confession has no right to love
—and the same is repeated:
love springs from the object.

You will be able to love it   only
the process   only.
      (Not proper love.)
Time understands that it happens
everyone, hatred as he does
it really seems to have been so.
      Research did not love
      about the significance
         he was indifferent.
Negative signs transformed into intellectual reality
lack divine is behind activity
climax when knowledge won
emotion praised language.
      A development, mode
example teaches   stormy consumes
      beyond love instead of loving.
            There are some further consequences.

II

Laws of light, colors, shadows and
perspective, the imitation of nature
the same value branches the subject
the proportions of the human body
vital functions become overwhelming
science was always something kept
away from him. Attempt to exercise
when there was little room.

He saw countless problems arising to see the work of art.
Most exhausting explanation: in the subject's early child
hood we make the place for example—instead of loving
we venture. There has been a sexual special intensity.
The curiosity of small children questions an end because
researches are directed to the question. Information, meaning serious
adults—
          inside the mother's body.

The period of infantile sexual
repression opens the whole of
the subject. Play by education
in this way gives an effective
impetus—the outbreak of a
        neurotic illness.

Color becomes
a solution.
Most perfect
unconscious desire—
research becomes
sexual activity.
Complete processes
are absent
—there operate
sexual themes.
Research homosexuality.

        The secret
        would appear
        a model
        in service
        of research.
        Some picture
        in years
        seems foolish
        for material
        when information
        escapes attention.

About youth we know very little.

A grave father in those days
fathers his mother probably
a girl married the only piece
of information comes from a
document of the household
of the marriage remained

childless.   little town
up in his father's house he
did not leave the house the
year name was already. That
                                is all.
            There is only one place.

Information about vultures suddenly interrupts
                memory. Very early sprung was
always vultures earliest memories was in my
vultures and opened my mouth many times
against my lips.
What have memory that a person should   memory
period is not impossible. Any means this   memory
namely that a vulture opened the child's mouth
with an end to fabulous difficulties. Our judgment
vultures memory. The vulture formed a date in
which memories originate. The moment of being
experienced and afterward repeated is already past
in the process of writing history.
            It was an age of historical writing
            not historians.

III

History of the past rather than
the past—wrong interpretation orders
motives for writing history,   mirroring
memories of his story about the vulture.
            Only time might be satisfied—
this story   to reject the body
            all the distortions and misunderstandings
the past, they are what forms
experience. In disclosing the historical
legendary material, he remembers childhood indifference.
            He himself does not understand
                                priceless pieces
the techniques of excellent light, concealed
so that many other studies have met no

better fate.   The eyes of the vulture
seem to recall examples from special language.
Familiar symbols in other languages—the situation
of a vulture beating vigorously the idea. A sexual
act   in which the penis
                    is put into the mouth.
Fantasy found women, passive homosexuals
who play the woman in. The reader will
                                        restrain
allow memory the very first time—
significance, in the most unambiguous fashion:
meaning, a dream, a vision, or delirium.
Analysis has not yet spoken   its last   word.

Sculptures, being in love, are found by doctors.

Difficulty informs satisfaction—the most innocent kind only repeats.
                    The most innocent kind only repeats.
Comfortable into our mouth and sucked at it
a penis resembles the stage and the shape, position
under the belly. Pleasure remains a familiar function.
Now we understand the memory of experience.
The vulture period is merely his mother
human beauty transformed into a passive homosexual
being the question of homosexuality
                    homosexual fact
—his mother, we find, his mother   the vulture
does it happen to be found?
Childhood is to separate memory
his mother the vulture was aware of his father his mother.
The fact of birth is in his vulture—himself, a vulture child
when that happened it is here. Mother with his poor absence
his father married a lady of good birth this marriage his
house. Disappointment had probably grown up an attractive
young boy.   The vulture of life
has elapsed of his mother
before he could   then it was too late.
The outside established memories are built on
            elements in his fact vulture

alone with his mother, was that the child
his early problem began with special sexual researches
—his curiosity, the vulture.
The vulture of his memory
the context, a bright light
against a homosexual situation.
The mother has been turned into a   vulture
in which language substitutes the   vulture
anything signifies a penis—understand activity.
The bird is a mother with a mark of masculinity
                           in view of this
                           absurdity we are
                           at a loss how to
                            reduce this to any
                           meaning.

We should despair
                  we reflect the past   we have
given up meaning.
Is there any reason why a memory should give us an explanation?
The fact is intended to embody the mother
which is the opposite of everything.
Sexual theories: when the mother
is dominated his body exists, all human beings
destroyed perception, he cannot find
a penis in girls, little girls had a penis but
it was cut off and in its place
was left a wound.
So dear under the influence of this threat
a new light will tremble for masculinity
despite unhappy creatures.
The cruel punishment has already fallen
complex women value intense desire
genitals culminate her.
The discovery of disgust becomes
        fetishistic reverence
                —puberty
leaves indelible traces
from primitive time.

Time suffers in the process.
Something more contained changed
        the mother is a situation
when we remember the historical homosexual
(having behaved as emotionally homosexual)
the question is forced upon existence
                —his mother is homosexuality.

We know the homosexual does exist
and in fact,   homosexual men
impose representing themselves.
Theoretically, being is a stage, a third sex:
they are,   they claim.
Men find pleasure in men and have been
                        in women.
Homosexuality offers homosexuals
but all so far have yielded
the same male homosexual subjects
a rule their mother.
Our intense childhood is afterwards forgotten
the father I have occasionally seen
the son made the correct object.
A transformation mechanism we do not yet understand
        succumbs to mother
he puts place with her
his model in the new objects.
        Love
grows up. Childhood
love finds the object.   Love—narcissism.
Reflection of everything changed the lovely name.
A man who becomes homosexual remains
in this way fixated on image.   His love
to pursue boys, the male object,   repeats
over.   His mother: the mechanism
(by which he acquired his homosexuality).

Homosexuality is quite obvious
homosexuals are not comprehensive
reasons called homosexuality may arise.

Processes process, but we know not what they are—
the particular process is homosexuality:
        we require what we cannot reject.

Our homosexual is unknown
homosexuality not usually traced
we should not have any cause for entering
                the form of homosexuality.

            The problem possible
            we require a strong vulture.

IV

We find anything untransformed
the homosexual, emphasized, allowed
                to be reckoned.
            He treated them with kindness and
            consideration, nursed them as a mother
            nurses her children—a mother chosen
            for her beauty.
Not for none of them
after his death they disappeared
history works like the diary of other mortals.
            Complete silence, quoted by biographers
                no record or any other evidence.
Bad habits
a pair of trousers and a jacket
my purse was never possible.
            Small weaknesses   behind vivid light
The death of the mother was
his mother. Process processes insignificant intensity
his act is performed in his mother's   funeral.
            He was to her erotically
                the subsequent love did not allow
                knowledge as something intelligible.

We have learnt the funeral.

                    Manner that his mother
                    betrayed erotic life.
His own objects dominated us.
Homosexuality succeeded in the emergence of
                            the situation.
Meaning was exactly that type.
                I became a homosexual.

We have not done with vulture
in words, many times against my lips.
Mother linking his mother the
vulture activity. The mouth zone—
a second memory.
This may be translated: my mother
is compounded—the memory
        of being and being his mother.
Nature has the artist from himself
(means he creates strangers)
emotion is nothing   witness memory
childhood something
impression before a work of art
        demonstration within anyone.
Female subjects produce the most   interpretation
erotic women between and between men
—ruthlessly demanding men as if they were alien beings.
He employed artifices.
We fancy lady taken:
the delicate details achieve the person
let us leave her smile
we cannot assume her face
        not herself, the conclusion
this model spells   this situation
                beheld   at last.

Something in him had an old memory
memory had never aroused his childhood
        his dreams literarily formed the subject.
            It is not intended to prove anything—
        some heads of laughing women

　　　　some children's heads were beautiful.
We learn a career of objects
we have　　　　　　　　　　　　the vulture.
Reproductions of his repetitions
begin to smile.　　　　　　　　His mother
had lost it when he found it again
　　　　　　　　　found it again in the lady.

V

Child is not possible
Composition—
in his mind the
memory of his　　　　　mother.
We may permit
less beautiful
treatment of
subjects. The　　　　　woman
plays unmistakably.
Mysterious quiet: known
versions. Perhaps
time draws　　　　　vulture.
In his house
he found details.
His mother was
these circumstances.

Childhood watched over
　　　　mother
who must have portrayed a young woman
—beauty has given the boy two mothers.
Smile the motherhood the same way
　　　　he had two mothers
he was between and tender. His mother was
his wife.　　　　　The design shapes him
earlier, she was

　　　　　　　she was forced to give
　　　　　　　up her son, the
unfortunate woman.

She had once given up a confirmation.
We find grown
the memory of his   mother
would to search and   suffer.
        Mother's privations were
the violence.
        He remained his vulture, was
only too natural.
Her memories forced her father to fondle
him.   Husband him of
his masculinity. She enjoyed no husband
like all unsatisfied mothers.
        She cares for something
                love represents
        satisfying impulses. Human happiness
must be called perverse.

VI

Aware the baby marriage
son becomes the rival
rapture played his mother
forbade desire from lips
reproduce his giving
fact into secret dares
penetrate the vulture.
Love denied unhappiness
representing his mother
—mother triumphed.
The boy in his female natures.

Error, the father
death of the sentence
time—repetition
already written
(at the beginning).
Nothing processes
he learnt ago
forgetting repetition

significant repetition—
an excellent means
of affective color.
My poor father
displacement died
all emotions.
A position—
his wives died
he married
his two daughters.
Father plays
psychosexual place
escape identity
gain house
his mother found
homosexuality
about puberty.
Sexual significance
kept erotic servants
responsibility for nothing
almost nothing
a copy—his father
his father, a gentleman
therefore never
never ceased to play
(to show what his
father really looks like).

A father created about them
father's concern
news died in a dungeon
someone of his father
the fact he was
in what he said.

Father damage against father
becomes the first modern
scientist. The man since
time. Teaching constantly

repeating. Man had already
forced the little boy.
We translate the mother
in most other human beings.
The existence of sexual father
by his father when everyone has
found unable to escape
father complex in father
parental complex. Biologically
speaking, father breaks down.
Child's ideas of them dates
childhood in attempts to deny
(illness is easily explained).

Astray, he calculated in hesitation
the last church made human
show lack for ultimate cause.
All these noble secrets:
human beings, subjects removed
from the world. Childhood
problems of sexuality
research transparent—problem
of birds, special attention.

The great bird will take the universe.

The art of himself—
he probably hoped we know
from dreams what bliss
is expected.
Why do so many people dream?
A bird is only a disguise for words:
a bridge—we recognize children
as a large bird. We find the phallus
as having wings.
The male organ   is called
the bird.
All these are fragments
from which we learn nothing.

VII

An adult happy time   children
          but if children themselves—
future, without any information.
          Grown-ups games—
aviation has infantile erotic
          form a special problem
the violent disguise of childhood.

          Maturity in mechanical sex
          —slight changes in meaning
          the same subject.
          Frustrated toys: he got
          a soft lump.
          He filled with air
          he made wings.
          He put it in a box and terrified
          friends carefully
          forced people to become transparent
          gradually became transparent and filled with air.
The room is illustrated by genius
the same playful form
devoid of example. Manuscripts
conclude while he was there.
          Play vanished from his childhood if in his childhood
the highest erotic bliss
                    is never again attained.

Blind the fact
all pathology
clothe things in him
—pretext and disguise
pathology does not, no one
should be blamed   never promised.
We discover special reasons: emotional
traces (smooth), life's struggles
human weakness, strange fact

regrettable fantasies, fascinating
secrets—penetrating his
love, his thirst.

      An attempt by learning from him
      we make sacrifices from childhood
      the awkward phrase never goes
nerve case   the light gained in the field
      the tragic mark of failure.
A human being substitute for
the practical concept of illness
place to what are known.
      Summarize the picture
art and science—these statements
provoked mysterious men.
Attraction
instinctual passions
      subdued a manner
(remarkably).
      The truth limits biography
      circumstances support physical mechanisms
the basis for his nature of reactions
      transformations explained: operation
of fate. Blame methods or material.
            The failure
to pronounce
could be dealt with
in no other way.
      The person had to maintain
      the accident.   His birth
      and his mother
      influence this phase   of childhood.
We must recognize
freedom which cannot be resolved.
      Means has no right to claim the consequence.
We are left with special instincts
—instincts in the foundation
      of mental character
the function

the tendency
                    intimacy we must admit
                          the male
we will not remain along that path.
A man renders manifestation
                        experiences of light
                        beauty based on a melancholy career
his achievements and misfortunes—
                    painted in the childhood fantasy
    of vulture.

In fact, everything lacks any connection with our wishes and illusions.
                        Our childhood
is no longer possible.
        The universe forces her way into experience.

Acknowledgments

Christopher Sweeney thanks Christian Hawkey, Anna Moschovakis, and Joshua Furst for their direction and support. He thanks Greg and Dave for their criticism and conversation; Kendall, Wadiah, Lisandre, and Seth for all of their help with this book. He thanks Robby and Chris for their friendship and all that that has entailed.

"The Mountain," being in print, is for Mr. Snyderman's father, Alan. He thanks the Canadian province of Quebec, the newly born Aradia Zorah Snyderman in California, his teachers in Brooklyn, and the publisher of this book, Seth Jani, who was the first poet in his life.

Lonely Christopher thanks Mr. Hawkey for putting on his six-breasted female wookie suit and smoking cigarettes with us on his porch while talking about taking baths in acid. He thanks Robert Fitterman and Anselm Berrigan for being his invisible friends. He thanks Jonathan Edwards for preaching the good word and being the perfect kidnap victim; Sigmund Freud for late night phone conversations with weird homoerotic undertones. He thanks everybody who contributed to facilitating this awkward and wonderful volume. He thanks Jen Hyde for tirelessness and charm. Most of all, he is eternally grateful to Sweeney and Bob—for the writing life.

Acknowledgements

About the Authors

Christopher Sweeney is an editor with The Corresponding Society, a press based in Brooklyn, New York.

Robert Snyderman was born in Pennsylvania. He grew up with two brothers in mind. He learned that he's a poet in Brooklyn beside Chris Sweeney and Lonely Christopher.
He learned how to be a poet while walking and hitch-hiking in North America. The Mountain took 11 months to write. It suffered a sea change in the town of L'Anse-au-Griffon in Gaspésie in Quebec where he lived with the woman who painted the front and back cover of this book. He is also a playwright. His most recent drama will be performed in theaters and on the streets in North America in Spring and Summer of the year 2010.

Lonely Christopher is the author of the short fiction collection *The Mechanics of Homosexual Intercourse* (Akashic, 2011); his chapbooks *Satan* and *Gay Plays* have been published by Small Anchor Press. His dramatic work includes an opera libretto, *Stegosaurus*, *Endymion Dreams the Moon*, and the *Gay Play* trilogy, which has been translated into Mandarin and produced and published in China. He is a founding member of the small press The Corresponding Society and the editor of its blog.
More info: www.thecorrespondingsociety.com/lonelychristopher.

About The Press

Seven CirclePress was founded in 2008 by New England poet Seth Jani. It publishes both online and off and aims to create a collective of the best voices from the independent literary scene.

It commits to no prescribed esthetic but has a strong inclination to view art as a means of promoting unity and meaningful interaction.

It has a strong online presence with the amount of visitors growing daily.

SCP publishes a select number of books/chapbooks a year as well as *CircleShow: The Official Journal Of Seven CirclePress*, released biannually.

www.ingramcontent.com/pod-product-compliance
Lightning Source LLC
Chambersburg PA
CBHW030149200626
46812CB00016B/1763